# GETTING THE BEST FROM THE BIBLE

SELWYN HUGHES

Published 2001 by CWR, Wavereley Abbey House, Waverley Lane, Farnham, Surrey, GU9 8EP, UK.
Registered charity No. 294387. Registered limited company No. 1990308.
Reprinted 2007, 2011.

Some of this material originally appeared in 1989 in *Getting the Best out of the Bible*, part of the Waverley Study Series.

Concept development, editing, design and production by CWR
Printed in the UK by Nuffield Press
ISBN: 978-1-85345-187-4

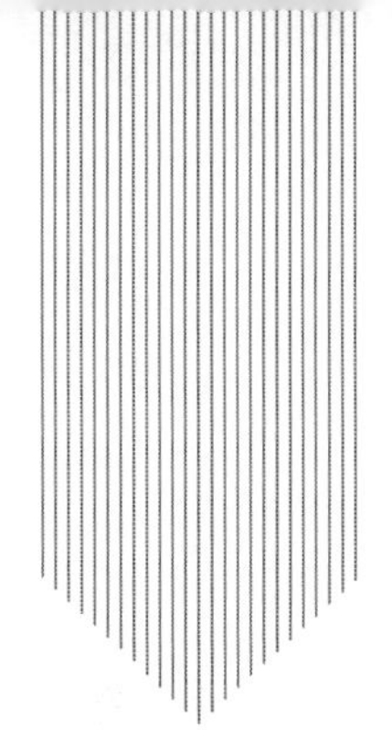

# Contents

*Blessed is the man*
*who does not walk in the counsel of the wicked*
*or stand in the way of sinners*
*or sit in the seat of mockers.*
*But his delight is in the law of the LORD,*
*and on his law he meditates day and night.*
*He is like a tree planted by steams of water,*
*which yields its fruit in season*
*and whose leaf does not wither.*
*Whatever he does prospers.*

**Psalm 1: 1-3**

# **Introduction** from Mick Brooks

The late Selwyn Hughes, founder of CWR, was passionate about helping people engage with the Bible in a meaningful way. Perhaps the best known vehicle for this passion was the Bible-reading devotional *Every Day with Jesus*, which he wrote every two months for over forty years, and which continues to be published today, ministering to nearly a million people worldwide.

Selwyn originally wrote *Getting the Best from the Bible* back in 1989 and it was revised in 2001. The copy you now hold in your hands is a new edition released especially for Biblefresh 2011, an initiative aimed at inspiring and equipping people to delve deeper into the Bible and let it 'change their world'. At CWR we are delighted that, in support of Biblefresh, we are able offer this publication once again. And we are so grateful to our dedicated supporters whose generous giving has made it possible for us to give it away free of charge to anyone who has a desire to 'delve into' Bible reading. There are also some special vouchers at the back of this edition to help you continue with your devotions.

This book focuses particularly on the subject of biblical meditation. In seeking to get the best from the Bible, biblical meditation is an important key. It is when we spend time alone with God and His Word, away from the noise and busyness of life, that we are able to uncover the life-transforming truths that the Bible offers. We hope and pray that through reading this book you will 'catch' some of Selwyn's passion for the Bible and will benefit from the wisdom of a man who sought to immerse Himself in God's Word.

Sincerely yours, in His name

**Mick Brooks**
Chief Executive of CWR

# **Introduction** from Selwyn Hughes

Biblical meditation is one of the most important keys to Christian living. Yet it is one of the most neglected – surprising, really, in view of the rich rewards God promises to those who practise it. This is what *Getting the Best from the Bible* is all about: teaching on this vital subject.

Meditation on the Scriptures is not a 'cure all'. It should not be seen as a substitute for other spiritual disciplines nor an escape from responsibilities. Those who benefit most from such meditation are those who are obedient – hence the emphasis in this book of applying what is being studied. When glaring violations of Scripture go uncorrected in a person's life the Bible will remain a closed book, no matter how much they try to meditate.

This does not mean you have to be perfect to discover the rewards of meditation, but it does mean that you have to have a willing and obedient heart. Throughout the ages the people of God have discovered that the more one obeys the Word of God the more light shines out from it.

There are several useful tools that can help you in biblical meditation. You need a Bible of course! And while one translation such as the New International Version is adequate it is good to have two or three other versions, including a paraphrase, to compare the rendering of Scripture passages. Most Bible versions are available online – for example on www.biblegateway.com. A Bible lexicon is helpful for understanding the original meaning of Scripture texts. A good concordance will help you find your way around the Bible. You might also find a topical Bible such as Nave's and a Bible dictionary well worth adding to your 'toolkit'. A visit to your local Christian bookshop could be profitable and point you in the right direction.

Whatever tools you choose to use with this study guide, my prayer is that through *Getting the Best from the Bible* God will do something dynamic in your Christian life and help you to walk closer with Him. I can guarantee that the hours you spend reading and meditating on the Scriptures will be the most profitable of your life.

**Selwyn Hughes**
**2001**

# About **Getting the Best from the Bible**

*Getting the Best from the Bible* presents the subject and principles of biblical meditation on a step-by-step basis over an eight-week period. Each week a particular aspect of biblical meditation is covered so that, progressively, the reader gains a firm understanding of the subject.

One of the best times to invest in this project is the time that already belongs to God – the Sabbath. This is why each week's study begins on Sunday the day when we are more readily focused on God and His Word.

Saturdays give the opportunity to review the week and complete an exercise particularly relevant to what has been learned during that week.

Something that many Christians would like to be able to do is to memorise Scripture verses to encourage themselves or others. To help you get into a habit of memorising Scripture *Getting the Best from the Bible* includes a memory verse for each week. The memorising is reinforced each day through the writing out of the verse in the space provided. You can also help ensure that the memory verse stays with you by writing it on one or more small pieces of card and put them in places where you will see them during the day – for example on your bathroom mirror, fridge door, in front of the kitchen sink, inside the car windscreen, on your desk, PC, as a bookmark …

To assist the reader each day, the material is set out using one of the main principles of discipleship: clear teaching of a particular point followed by the opportunity for the reader to apply or respond to what has been taught.

## The daily layout includes:

**TEACHING WITH THOUGHT FOR THE DAY**

Commentary to reflect on. This leads to

**ACTION**

A Scripture reading and/or exercise. This leads to

**REACTION**

The opportunity to write down your own thoughts and response

**PRAYER**

WEEK 1

# A JOURNEY OF DISCOVERY

WEEK 1

## DAY 1 | Sunday

# This is the beginning of one

of the most important journeys you can ever set out on: to discover the lost art of biblical meditation. Biblical meditation is the one certain way of maintaining spiritual peace, poise and purpose, yet many Christians dismiss meditation as an Eastern religions thing. David Ray, a writer and minister, used to think Christians who promoted Bible meditation were out of touch with reality. His attitude was, 'Give me action and work – lots of work. Let someone else waste time staring at the end of his nose.' But when someone introduced him to the principles of biblical meditation he soon became more aware of God's presence than ever before.

As we go on our journey of discovery let this and every Sabbath be, as much as possible, the day of rest and reflection God means it to be. Church activities are important, but so is being alone with the Lord. Find time to be still and meditate on God's goodness and beauty. You will find it time well spent. Jesus did.

**This week's Memory Verse is**

> *'Be still, and know that I am God'*
> **PSALM 46:10**

Write it down and find time today to let it sink into your heart.

---

---

---

This week you will learn something of the vast difference between biblical meditation and other forms of meditation, the important part played by God's Spirit in meditation and, most important of all, how Jesus is at the heart of it all. Happy travelling!

# DAY 2 | Monday

To get the best from the Bible we must be clear about its central message – the incarnation – Jesus coming into our world in human form. Some regard the Bible as a book they can delve into for magic formulas and facts. The Bible is not a book of magic but a moral revelation. It shows us that through the incarnation God invades humanity with incorrigible love. We do not have to find God – we simply let God find us. If you miss your way here you will come to wrong conclusions about God, life and salvation. In receiving Jesus we are one with God. Having been brought into a relationship with the Almighty through faith in His Son, we are then ready to increase our knowledge of the living Word through, and by, the written Word.

If we try to build up our personalities from any other starting point than Jesus we will be like those of whom it is described:

*They sail away on a sea of mist*
*To a land that doesn't exist*

*'The Word became flesh ...'*

'Much light will yet break out from the Word of God, especially if the "Word of God" is the Word of God – "the Word made Flesh,"' said Pastor Robinson, who ministered to the Pilgrim Fathers. Transcendental meditation and New Age type cults seek to get converts to empty their minds to find God. Christianity encourages converts to fill their thoughts with God, especially the Almighty's highest thought – Jesus.

**Thought for Today**

The more I think God's highest thought the more I will know Him.

## Action

**READ JOHN 6:25-35.**

Write out and think about verse 35

How much are you allowing Jesus to feed your life?

## Reaction

My thoughts, notes and prayers

## Prayer

**Father God, thank You for Jesus becoming flesh and that His coming is the central message of the Bible. With this key in my heart I look forward to knowing more about You as I learn to meditate on Your Word, guided by the Holy Spirit. Amen.**

## Memory Verse

Write out this week's verse and reference

## DAY 3 | Tuesday

It must be emphasised that when there was nothing we could do to climb up to God, Almighty God came down to us in the Person of His Son, Jesus Christ. This fact lies at the heart of the Bible and is the key to opening up its treasures. If you miss this you will miss the focal point of revelation and fail to fully benefit from Scripture meditation.

The Bible progressively uncovers as much of God's nature as we are able to understand. God's final and perfect revelation is seen in Jesus: the incarnation is the revelation. Everything else develops from this point. Where the emphasis on the incarnation is weak the sense of revelation is weak and people go off into all kinds of 'revelations' that, in reality, amount to nothing more than fantasies. They discover 'Christ within themselves' – which turns out to be a Christ of their own creation. The characteristics of Jesus, only begotten Son of God and crucified, ascended Saviour of the world, fade out and a weak, sentimental Christ takes His place.

That's why there can be no place for New Age or transcendental meditation and the like in the Christian Church. 'Leave your mind at the door' said a notice at the entrance to one New Age type meeting. Christianity, in contrast, encourages converts to fill their minds with God's thoughts. And God's highest thought is Jesus.

**Thought for today**

I read books to get light.
I read *the* Book to get
*the* Light.

## Action

The Bible is God's message to man, not man's message to God. If the Bible is merely a collection of interesting writings about God it cannot be viewed as the final authority for life. The truth is that God, not men, initiated and inspired the Scriptures – the Almighty coming down to us, not us climbing up to Him.

Consider this as you read **2 Peter 1:16-21** and praise God for taking the initiative!

## Reaction

My thoughts, notes and prayers

______________________________

______________________________

______________________________

## Prayer

**Dear Lord, thank You that You came down to me through Your Son, Jesus, instead of leaving me to struggle by my own fruitless efforts to climb up to You. I am so grateful for such a wonderful key to unlock the revelation of Your Word. Amen.**

## Memory Verse

Write out this week's verse and reference

______________________________

______________________________

## DAY 4 | Wednesday ________________

# The Christian life is one of progress – in spiritual maturity, of getting to know God better and better, of being more aware, more sensitive to His presence and His ways. One of the most effective ways is through biblical meditation. Notice I say *biblical* meditation, for there are many forms of meditation that claim to lead people to God but which, in fact, lead them away from Him.

The only way a person can know God is through a personal encounter with Jesus Christ. The glorious message of the Bible is summed up in the fact that when there was nothing we could do to climb up to God, the Almighty God became the Son of Man in order that the sons of men might become the sons of God.

The Bible is the only way through which Christians can increase their understanding and awareness of God. Biblical meditation, along with an understanding of the power of God, will keep us from erring. Some Christians make the mistake of wholly concentrating on the Scriptures – past revelation – and ignore the power of the Holy Spirit who gives revelation from the Word: what God wants to say to us *now*. Others have experienced the power of the Spirit in their life and experience but do not know the Scriptures in any real sense. They too err, for we cannot correctly discern God at work in our lives and churches unless we continually check spiritual experiences with the revelation contained in the Scriptures.

**Thought for today**

The abiding presence of the Holy Spirit enables us to understand Scripture as God meant it.

## Action

The Bible can only be properly interpreted when the reader is indwelt by the Holy Spirit.

**Read 1 Corinthians 2:1-16** and write out verse 14 below.

How does this explain why so many brilliant minds stumble over truths in the Bible that are crystal clear to the youngest Christian convert?

## Reaction

My thoughts, notes and prayers

## Prayer

**Thank You, Father, for the Bible and for the power of the Holy Spirit who makes Your Word come alive and speaks to me today. Help me as I meditate and allow the Spirit to show me what You are saying. Amen.**

## Memory Verse

Write out this week's verse and reference

# DAY 5 | Thursday

Two men were travelling by ship. One began each day of the voyage by eagerly picking up the daily news-sheet and turning to the stock market report. If prices were up his face lit up. If they were down he looked down. The other man, a Christian missionary, began his day differently. He leaned over the rail each morning reading the Bible and then looked out over the open sea in meditation. His face always had a calm expression. His happiness did not depend on what was happening, but on an awareness of God that was not subject to the changing circumstances of time.

We must allow the Bible to direct our thinking – otherwise our moods will go up and down like the man concerned about the stock market. Unless we anchor our lives on the Scriptures we will be tossed around by every circumstance we encounter.

Some Christians seek God without seeking Him in His Word. 'I know of a devoted Christian who comes into his Quiet Time without a Bible and just sits in meditation', wrote Dr Stanley Jones in one of his books. 'He thinks he can come to God direct. But does he? He gets to God through the medium of his own conceptions of God. His conceptions are man's thoughts of God. So my friend is an unstable Christian. He is subject to his own moods. He is self-centred instead of Scripture-centred.' Our thoughts need to be constantly corrected by God's thoughts – through His Word.

**Thought for today**

The best news to begin the day with is found in God's Word.

## Action

**READ PSALM 63:1-11**

Think about what you start your day with. How does it affect the way you think and act in the hours that follow? Do you need to change your start-of-the-day routine to become more Scripture-centred?

Write out your response to this challenge below.

## Reaction

My thoughts, notes and prayers

## Prayer

**Dear Father, help me to absorb Your Word so deeply that it governs the way I think and all I do – whatever the circumstances I encounter in life. Amen.**

## Memory Verse

Write out this week's verse and reference

# DAY 6 | Friday

Many people read the Bible, study the Bible, memorise the Bible and yet fail to get the best from it because they miss the biggest single secret of making the Bible come alive in their life and experience – *meditation.* For some reason biblical meditation has been largely lost to the modern Church. It desperately needs to be rediscovered. In this increasingly unstable world it cannot be stressed enough that the one sure way of maintaining spiritual peace and poise is through daily meditation on God's Word.

Biblical meditation is so much different from meditation practised by the gurus of Eastern religions and their followers because we absorb God's thoughts, not our own. At the heart of the Bible's message is Jesus. Biblical meditation is different from reading, studying and memorising the Bible. The former are primarily intellectual exercises that bring spiritual results, but meditation is a way in which the Word of God is carried direct to our spirit, where He can accomplish the great work of transforming our lives. The spirit is the centre of our personality, the motivating force. The Bible sometimes speaks of it as the 'heart'.

The Bible contains words and sayings which when meditated upon yield tremendous spiritual power. Our Lord knew Scripture so well that He was able to use it to overcome and defeat Satan. Three times He resisted Satan by quoting the precise words that were necessary to rebut the temptation. This is one of the most important reasons for biblical meditation.

**Thought for today**

Nothing can stand when it comes up against the power of God's Word.

## Action

**READ EPHESIANS 6:10-18**

Write out verse 17 and soak in the truth that we can use the precise sayings of Scripture to combat Satan's power and create within us new desires that will be in harmony with God's will and purpose for our lives.

___

___

___

Is there a specific situation in your life which needs the application of the Word of God?

Can you find a scripture which gives God's answer to your situation?

If you need help use a concordance or ask help from someone you can trust.

My thoughts, notes and prayers

___

___

___

## Prayer

**Dear God, thank You that Your Word is a powerful weapon. Help me both to absorb more of it and use it for Your glory. Amen.**

## Memory Verse

Write out this week's verse and reference

___

___

# DAY 7 | Saturday

It's a week since we began our journey into meditating on the Bible – one of the greatest journeys a Christian can make. During that time we have found that:

- Biblical meditation teaches us about God's nature, especially His totally undeserved grace and forgiveness through sending Jesus – 'the Word made flesh'. The incarnation is the central message of the Bible.
- Meditating in the Scriptures is different from meditation practices of Eastern religions because through it we absorb God's thoughts, not our own. God's highest thought is Jesus.
- An understanding of the power of the Holy Spirit is essential to biblical meditation. The Spirit gives us true revelation from the Word. God's Word and God's Spirit together will keep us from error.
- Biblical meditation keeps us on an even keel despite our circumstances – affecting the way we think and act.
- Biblical meditation is far more beneficial than reading, studying and memorising the Scriptures. The latter are primarily spiritual exercises that bring spiritual results, but through meditation the Spirit takes His Word direct to our hearts and transforms our lives through it.
- Meditating on the Scriptures is a powerful defence against the attacks and wiles of Satan – as Jesus vividly demonstrates.

## Action

To meditate on the Bible we must have total confidence that it is the inspired, authoritative Word of God. The Bible is a moral revelation – not some magical formula. Look up the scriptures listed on the next page and then answer the questions.

### Thought for today

This week I have started a journey of life-transforming discovery.

**1 THESSALONIANS 2:13; MATTHEW 4:4; PROVERBS 3:5; MATTHEW 5:17; PSALM 138:2; MALACHI 3:6; 2 TIMOTHY 3:16**

Whose idea was it to put together the words of the Bible?

Is every word of the original manuscripts pure and free from error?

Why is it so important to read, study and meditate on the Bible regularly?

How high a priority does God put on His Word?

Does God's Word change to meet the needs of succeeding generations?

How much of the Bible is 'God-breathed'?

Did Christ abolish the Old Testament?

Did the Early Church believe in the inspiration of Scripture?

## Reaction

My thoughts, notes and prayers

## Prayer

**Dear heavenly Father, I look back with grateful thanks to You for what I have learned in these past few days about meditating on Your Word. Please teach me more. Amen.**

## Memory Verse

Write out this week's verse and reference

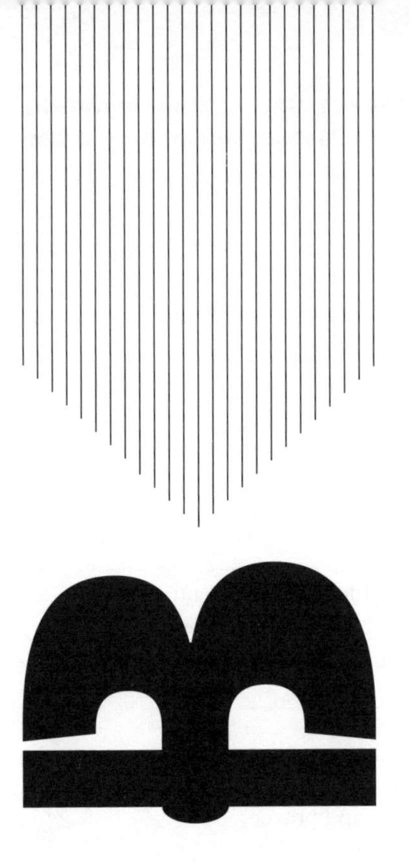

WEEK 2

# THE PURPOSES OF BIBLICAL MEDITATION

# DAY 1 | Sunday

What does biblical meditation actually *achieve*? you may well be asking at this stage of our journey. This is the question I shall be addressing during this second week: exploring areas of our lives that God wants to change and only can as we invest time in meditating in His Word. We will explore how He realigns our personalities to live according to His will and purposes. We will see how absorbing the Scriptures can radically change our thought life and transform our emotions, making us more and more *God*-centred and less and less *self*-centred.

We shall also look at the vitally important issue of making *time* to meditate, but for a start it would be good to re-evaluate our Sundays – the *Lord's* Day. God's plan for the Jewish nation was that they did their work in six days so that they would be able to give God the seventh day in 'delighting themselves in the Lord'. 'Nearly all the ills of life spring from this simple source, that we are not able to sit still in a room,' declared Pascal, the famous French philosopher. What if our Sabbath was more still? It would have a calming and healing influence on our lives.

We will be looking further how to establish regular times to spend with God over His precious Word at the end of this week after exploring what He wants to do in us through meditation.

## This week's Memory Verse is

> *'Trust in the LORD with all your heart and lean not on your own understanding'*
> **PROVERBS 3:5**

Write it down and use it as a starting point for biblical meditation today and throughout the week.

## DAY 2 | Monday

# Meditation is designed

by God to bring about major changes in our personality, especially our thoughts, feelings and decisions. Having 'rescued us from the dominion of darkness and brought us into the kingdom of the Son he loves, in whom we have redemption, the forgiveness of sins' (Col. 1:13–14), God wants to change us to be more and more like Jesus, and meditation is a key part of this process.

Since the fall of Adam and Eve in the Garden of Eden the human personality has been thrown out of line. So it badly needs readjustment and realignment. Original sin took place when Satan, instead of attempting to put pressure on Eve's will to take the forbidden fruit, simply dropped an insinuating doubt into her mind. He knew only too well that God had built the personality in such a way that what a human believes affects the way they act. Our thoughts affect our emotions and our emotions affect our decisions. Instead of rejecting the doubt Satan dropped into her mind, Eve allowed it to mingle with her thoughts and the doubt quickly led to her disbelieving in God – and eventually to disobeying God.

So from that day to this our natural mind has been directly contrary to God's principles. This means that every thought needs to be brought into line with God's thoughts. We do this through continual and persistent biblical meditation, getting to know His thoughts, principles and purposes.

### Thought for today

The best way to think is the way God thinks.

## Action

**READ ROMANS 11:33–12:2**

Ask yourself: What, generally, are my waking thoughts? How do they compare with God's thoughts? How do my thoughts need to be brought in line with His thoughts?

Write your answers below.

## Reaction

My thoughts, notes and prayers

## Prayer

**Dear Heavenly Father, I see that I need to saturate my thoughts with Your thoughts and fill my mind with Your truth. Help me to do this continually. Amen.**

## Memory Verse

Write out this week's verse and reference

WEEK 2

# DAY 3 | Tuesday

We are seeing that God has three main purposes in encouraging us to meditate: 1 – The reconstruction of our thoughts. 2 – The refocusing of our emotions. 3 – The realignment of our wills. Today we take a close look at the second. Even after our conversion to Christ our emotions still continue to manifest 'un-Christian' feelings – anger, bitterness, resentment, jealousy, envy, guilt and many others. We have already seen that our emotions are directly linked to our thoughts so that when we think right we feel right. If we could think as God thinks we would feel as God feels.

I have no doubt that when we bring our thoughts into line with God's thoughts through biblical meditation we are going to experience a radical transformation in our emotions. In a church I once pastored a lady said to me, 'My emotions are dulled and deadened. I can feel nothing – joy or sorrow, elation or despair. I have been so hurt that it is impossible for me to respond with feeling to anyone – even God.' She had experienced many difficulties in her life but I encouraged her to begin meditating. Within three months she had changed beyond recognition. She could laugh, cry, sing and display her emotions in a healthy and positive way.

This transformation had happened because the power of God's Word, mingling continually with her thoughts, began to filter through to her emotions and refocus them to operate as God intended. Meditation releases our emotions to express God's love.

**Thought for today**

With God in charge of my emotions I am emotionally balanced.

## Action

**READ PSALM 39**

How would you describe your emotional state? In what areas of your emotions in particular do you need God's transforming power?

Write down your response below.

## Reaction

My thoughts, notes and prayers

## Prayer

**Father God, I am realising how much my thoughts affect my emotions. Please do Your transforming work as I meditate on Your Word. Amen.**

## Memory Verse

Write out this week's verse and reference

## DAY 4 | Wednesday ___________________

# Doing the will of God is very

much dependent on transformed emotions. There are three views we can take of our emotions: as our enemies, our masters or our servants. Those who view them as enemies tend to repress them and live on a bomb – likely to explode at any moment. People who see their emotions as masters allow themselves to be pulled and pushed by negative feelings. The proper way to view emotions is as our servants – to do our bidding and serve our highest interests.

Our emotions become more and more subservient as we spend time exposing our thought life to God's Word through meditation. Because God designed our personalities they function best when He indwells them. My mind and God's thoughts were made for each other – not to be alien. Jesus said that *'Man does not live on bread alone, but on every word that comes from the mouth of God.'* As the stomach and food are made for each other we are fashioned in our inner natures for the will of God as expressed in His words. Notice that it says *every* word. A human personality thrives when it lives on every word that comes from God but perishes when it lives by every word from the mouth of hate, greed, fear …

When we meditate on God's Word and bring His thoughts into our mind our emotions recognise their Master's voice, come to attention before Him and are ready to do His bidding. Life only works God's way.

---

**Thought for today**

God's will is written in His Word and meditating on it brings peace.

## Action

**READ MATTHEW 4:1-11**

How much are you living by every word that comes from the mouth of God? What are the negative words that your life is influenced by?

Write your response, thoughts and remedial steps to take below.

## Reaction

My thoughts, notes and prayers

## Prayer

**O God, help me to fill my mind with Your Word so that my emotions can function in the way You designed them to. Amen.**

## Memory Verse

Write out this week's verse and reference

# DAY 5 | Thursday

Now we will take a close look at the third reason why God encourages us to meditate: realignment of our wills. The will responds to feelings and feelings respond to thoughts. We generally choose what makes us feel good – in line with our basic assumptions and thinking. From the moment each of us enters this world our will responds to the basic egocentricity within us. We want what we want when we want it.

Conversion to Christ means that the will has to be trained to respond to God's directions and purposes, but it cannot be trained unless those directions and purposes are stored in our memory through meditation.

Many Christians regard the Christian life as simply a battle of the will. They get up every morning gritting their teeth and with the attitude that they must strive as hard as they can to please God and do everything He wants them to do that day. No wonder that they fall back into bed at night utterly exhausted and frustrated! Instead of trying to conquer a rebellious will by forcing it to obey God's commands, flood your mind with God's Word by systematic meditation. The more you think God's thoughts the more your emotions delight in Him and you will want to obey Him more and more. When the mind is taught to think God's thoughts in meditation it is not long before the rest of the personality follows the same pattern – and feels and acts in response to right thinking.

**Thought for today**

Realignment of my will means becoming God-centred not self-centred.

## Action

**READ HOSEA 8:1-14**

As you meditate on this passage pay particular attention to verse 12. What is your attitude to aligning your will with God's ways? Are there any of His ways from which you shy away?

Write down your response to this challenge below, together with a re-commitment, if necessary, to seeking and doing His will.

## Reaction

My thoughts, notes and prayers

## Prayer

**Dear Father, I see that when my will clashes with Your will it brings conflict. Help my will to be in accord with Your will. Amen.**

## Memory Verse

Write out this week's verse and reference

## DAY 6 | Friday

**Having explored** God's purposes in encouraging us to meditate on His Word we need to look again at the important aspect of when to meditate, to make time to be alone to soak in what He is saying through the Scriptures. Dr Alexis Carrel pinpoints the problem by saying that 'We have lost the art in this modern age of developing "islands of solitude"'.

The home is the obvious place to meditate – during times of leisure and relaxation. Outdoors, too, while walking to and from work or school, for instance. Select a verse of Scripture and do the same as the great Baptist preacher, Charles Spurgeon: 'Whenever I go for a walk I take a verse of Scripture as I would a sweet on the end of my tongue and suck every precious drop of sweetness from it.'

Another time and place to meditate is at night when you get into bed. Before you go to sleep hold a portion of God's Word in your mind. Someone described it as 'giving God the night key to our hearts'. Go to sleep meditating on the Scriptures and you will find that His words *'when you sleep ... will watch over you'* (Prov. 6:22). This will make a tremendous difference when you wake up to begin a new day. If your last thought at night has been something from the Word of God then it will work during your subconscious (sleeping) hours and speak right back to you when you awake.

### Thought for today

God's words can work in me whether I am awake or asleep.

## Action

**READ PROVERBS 6:12-35**

Ask yourself: Can I find more times during the day or night to meditate on God's Word? Write down your findings below and begin today to meditate during the times you have discovered are available.

## Reaction

My thoughts, notes and prayers

---

---

---

## Prayer

**Lord, forgive me for the minutes and hours I waste every day that could be used in building up my spiritual resources. Help me to be alert to every opportunity to meditate on Your Word. Amen.**

## Memory Verse

Write down this week's verse and reference

---

---

---

WEEK 2

# DAY 7 | Saturday

We are at the end of our second week into our journey of discovery about biblical meditation. I hope that you are excited about what you have learned so far and eager to press on! This past week we have been looking at the reasons why God is so keen that His children spend time meditating on His Word:

- So that God can transform our thought life, refocus our emotions and realign our wills so that we not only do His will but delight in doing it. Because our emotions are linked to our thoughts we feel right once we allow Him to deal with our thoughts. Through meditation our emotions are released to express His love.
- Many Christians are caught in the treadmill of daily gritting their teeth to do God's will. Such attempts to conquer our rebellion will leave us exhausted. The way to victory is flooding our minds with God's thoughts through systematic Scripture meditation.
- Doing God's will depends on transformed emotions. The key to this is that our emotions become our servants – and more and more subservient through exposing our thought life to God's Word through meditation. God states that we should live on His *every* word.
- We have examined the need to put time aside to meditate, looking at ways to create 'islands of solitude'. We also need to practise meditating on Scripture before we go to sleep – so that His Word does its work in our subconscious hours.

## Thought for Today

Time well spent is with God through His Word.

## Action

**READ EPHESIANS 5:8-17**

Especially ponder J.B. Phillips' rendering of verses 16–17: *'Make the best use of your time, despite all the evils of these days. Don't be vague but grasp firmly what you know to be the will of the Lord.'* Write your thoughts and prayers below.

Who, or what, has first place in your life? Examine your priorities. Is your day built around your time with God or is time with God built around your day? Fill in the chart on page 37 so that you might be able to pinpoint exactly how your time is spent in an average week.

## Reaction

My thoughts, notes and prayers

## Prayer

**Dear Lord, help me from now on to build my time around You each day. Amen.**

## Memory Verse

Write down this week's verse and reference

## ESTABLISHING YOUR OWN PRIORITIES

The purpose of the chart is to enable you to evaluate the best use of your time. Fill in the spaces, indicating exactly what you did for each hour period. It is important to record *what you did*, not what you intended to do or should have done.

---

## CONCLUSION:

Now you have filled in the chart, what do you conclude? Are you giving adequate time to the cultivation and development of your spirit and soul? Make a note of anything you have to do to re-establish or rearrange your spiritual priorities.

### IN ORDER TO GIVE TIME TO BIBLICAL MEDITATION I MUST:

1. ______________________________

2. ______________________________

3. ______________________________

4. ______________________________

5. ______________________________

| | 12-5 | 5-6 | 6-7 | 7-8 | 8-9 | 9-10 | 10-11 | 11-12 | 12-1 | 1-2 | 2-3 | 3-4 | 4-5 | 5-6 | 6-7 | 7-8 | 8-9 | 9-10 | 10-11 | 11-12 |
|---|---|---|---|---|---|---|---|---|---|---|---|---|---|---|---|---|---|---|---|---|
| **SUN** | | | | | | | | | | | | | | | | | | | | |
| **MON** | | | | | | | | | | | | | | | | | | | | |
| **TUES** | | | | | | | | | | | | | | | | | | | | |
| **WEDS** | | | | | | | | | | | | | | | | | | | | |
| **THURS** | | | | | | | | | | | | | | | | | | | | |
| **FRI** | | | | | | | | | | | | | | | | | | | | |
| **SAT** | | | | | | | | | | | | | | | | | | | | |

WEEK 3

# THE REWARDS OF BIBLICAL MEDITATION

WEEK 3

# DAY 1 | Sunday ________

A family was living on the edge of the desert. One day they were amazed to see that seeds had been planted in the salty desert sands behind their home. They couldn't understand how this had happened because all their attempts to cultivate vegetables and flowers had failed. The mystery was eventually solved when one of them realised that the mother had been throwing her dishwater out of the back door. After months and months of this the salt, which hindered growth, had been washed out of the sand. One day the mother threw away some seeds, but because they fell where the water had drenched the ground they began to sprout and grow. If we saturate our minds with the Scriptures, all thoughts opposed to God's Word will be washed out and our spiritual lives will grow and bear the fruit He intended.

This week we will be exploring the rewards that committed biblical meditation brings. This will include a look at it through the life and example of Joshua, a leader totally committed to serving the Lord. The world desperately needs many such leaders today, especially in politics and business. Perhaps you could make time this Sabbath to pray about this (1 Timothy 2:1–4 will help you). Our studies will show us how meditation increases our understanding of right and wrong, of the superiority of God's 'higher education' over the world's approach to, and use of, knowledge. Are you ready to press on?

**This week's Memory Verse will help our focus:**

> *'... Christ loved the church and gave himself up for her, to make her holy, cleansing her by the washing with water through the word ...'*
>
> **EPHESIANS 5:25-26**

Write it down and use it as a starting point for biblical meditation today and throughout the week.

WEEK 3

# DAY 2 | Monday

## One of the first rewards

to be gained from meditating in the Scriptures is success. The book of Joshua narrates one man's success and contains important principles for our encouragement. Joshua was a man of proven character and ability. This resulted in him being one of only three adults to survive 40 years of wilderness wandering, after God's judgment on Israel's disobedience, to lead a nation of several million people across the flood-swollen river Jordan to settle in their promised land. When God took Moses away the reigns of leadership passed to Joshua. And what a leader he became!

In a brilliant, divinely inspired move, Joshua skilfully divided Canaan in half and then systematically defeated the southern armies before marching north to overcome the remaining occupants of the land. During the seven-year period the book of Joshua covers, the 12 tribes of Israel defeated 31 armies and captured 20 cities. The secret of Joshua's outstanding success was meditation. The continual inner mental and spiritual discipline of meditation gave Joshua clarity of thought, sharpness and intellect and a greater power of concentration. And Joshua had just a fragment of what is now available to us.

Do you want to be successful? Commit yourself to systematic meditation of God's Word. Do you long for successful leaders in the Church and in the life of the nation, especially politics and business? Pray for men and women living in His Word to occupy positions of power.

**Thought for today**

The path to victory
is through God's Word.

## Action

**READ JOSHUA 1:1-9**

When Joshua sought the Lord in meditation what did God do to him? What inspires you about Joshua's life? How would you describe God's definition of success compared with what society considers are the keys to success? Write down your response below.

## Reaction

My thoughts, notes and prayers

______________________________

______________________________

______________________________

## Prayer

**Dear Lord, I am realising that true success only comes when I learn to meditate on Your Word. Amen.**

## Memory Verse

Write out this week's verse and reference

______________________________

______________________________

______________________________

______________________________

# DAY 3 | Tuesday

Having seen that one of the rewards of meditating on the Word of God is true success we now examine another benefit: understanding. By this I mean the special insight God gives to those who meditate on the Scriptures, enabling them to discern more than secular authorities. The world gains its understanding of life through observation, experience and the acquiring of knowledge. The Christian who meditates, however, is given an awareness of the principles that govern the moral universe. There are many philosophies propounded today, so unless we can see through these faulty systems, recognising them for what they are, we will never experience a joyous life.

Understanding has been defined as 'the right application of knowledge'. Much of the knowledge gained by today's society is directly opposed to God's eternal principles. The world, for example, believes that the way to greatness is to become a leader. No, says Jesus, 'whoever wants to become great among you must be your servant' (Matt. 20:26).

There are benefits in secular education but we need to realise that while it ministers to the needs of the mind it fails to minister to the needs of the spirit. Much of secular education is anti-God anyway. Evolution is taught as fact and denies that the origins of life came from a supreme Creator – God. Sex education promotes immorality. By contrast, God has provided a 'higher' education for those who are truly His. In His school of meditation we gain more understanding than our teachers (Psa. 119:99).

### Thought for today

The way to greatness
is to bend low before God.

## Action

**READ MATTHEW 23:1-12**

What does this passage teach you about true understanding? Does this change your view of knowledge? What philosophies and practices directly opposed to God come to mind?

Write down your answers below.

## Reaction

My thoughts, notes and prayers

## Prayer

**Father, I enrol in Your school of 'higher' education. Help me to become a real meditator of Your Word. Amen.**

## Memory Verse

Write down this week's verse and reference

## DAY 4 | Wednesday

Another way we gain from meditation is we become able to discern between right and wrong: 'I have hidden your word in my heart that I might not sin against you' (Psa. 119:11). God appeared to Solomon and told him he could have anything he wanted. Solomon's response was to ask for 'an understanding heart … that I may discern between good and bad' (1 Kings 3:9, AV). This request pleased God so much that He not only gave Solomon wisdom and understanding but riches and honour as well. The ability to discern between right and wrong is an important part of our spiritual development and comes about mainly through exposure to the Word of God.

When we read and meditate in the Scriptures, God uses the Word hidden in our hearts to show us when our thoughts, actions and attitudes are displeasing to Him.

Failure to meditate in the Scriptures is one of the major reasons why so many Christians live barren and unfruitful lives. Psalm 1 explains that the secret of a spiritually fruitful life is to send one's roots down into the Word of God by meditation. As we do this we draw upon the life of God in His Word that, in turn, produces the spiritual fruitfulness the Bible everywhere encourages us to reveal. The picture is of a tree planted by the river, bringing forth fruit in its season and whose leaves never wither. Can you say that this is a picture of your Christian life?

### Thought for today

When I put down roots in His Word God waters them.

## Action

**READ PSALM 119:17-24**

What 'wonderful things' has God shown you since you started this journey of learning to meditate on His Word? Write your thoughts down below. Also write down verse 24, ponder it and memorise it.

## Reaction

My thoughts, notes and prayers

______________________________________________

______________________________________________

______________________________________________

## Prayer

**Dear Lord, help me to daily tap into Your life and power that pulses through Your Word. Amen.**

## Memory Verse

Write down this week's verse and reference

______________________________________________

______________________________________________

______________________________________________

______________________________________________

WEEK 3

## DAY 5 | Thursday

We have been seeing that as we meditate in the Scriptures God promises that we will grow in the areas of successful living, understanding, discerning the difference between right and wrong and becoming spiritually fruitful and prosperous. Another reward through meditation is discovering how to live. We know everything about life except how to live it. Conversion to Christ does not automatically give us this ability, for we will never know how to live effectively until we learn to tap, through meditation, into the resources God has deposited in the Bible. We do, of course, draw the life of God into our spirits through personal prayer, but prayer by itself is not enough. To live effectively we must saturate our thoughts with His Word.

Through meditating on the Scriptures we experience a heightening of all the powers of the personality, enabling us to gain a degree and quality of life that is divine. The mind becomes keener, the emotions become broader and more sensitive, and our will becomes more active and decisive.

The great statement of Augustine, though oft-quoted, is worth repeating here: 'Thou hast made us for thyself and our hearts are restless until they find their rest in thee.' Let it be burnt into your mind that meditation is the key that gives you access to God's treasures of life and power.

---

**Thought for today**

God's Word is the greatest treasure I can find.

## Action

**READ PROVERBS 4:1-13**

Write down your own wording of verse 4 below, together with the things in your life that He is challenging you to bring in line with His Word.

## Reaction

My thoughts, notes and prayers

## Prayer

**Dear Lord, help me to make Your Word more and more my treasure. I look forward to seeing more and more of its riches. Amen.**

## Memory Verse

Write out this week's verse and reference

# DAY 6 | Friday

Another of the benefits of meditation is that it helps us to memorise Scripture. The more we chew on it, talk to Jesus about it and apply it to our daily life the more likely we are to remember it. Seek to make Scripture part of you so that it is in your heart rather than just in your head. Unbelievers can memorise Scripture, too, even to the point of quoting the whole of the New Testament word for word – but without having one word in their hearts.

There are ways in which we can be helped to memorise Scripture. Having an image is important. The mind functions with images. It needs pictures and likenesses to be able to recall. Jesus knew that, which is why He used parables in His teaching. Spiritual truths and thoughts need to have a physical likeness to be remembered. The word parable comes from a root word meaning 'to throw or lay beside; to compare' – an aid to understanding and remembering. Psalm 23, for example, could be understood and remembered through visualising it as the psalmist saw it – the pasture, water, rod, staff and so on.

Once learned, Scripture verses and passages need to be retained. Keep on going back to them – repetition and review will keep what you have learned fresh in your mind. If you never review you will forget. This is not because you necessarily have a poor memory but through not returning to Scripture again and again your mind is saying that memorising is not important. But nothing could be further from the truth!

**Thought for today**

Scripture is so important that I must keep on thinking about it.

## Action

**READ DEUTERONOMY 11:18-22**

Think especially about verse 19: the word 'teach' here means to do something again and again – like sharpening a knife or polishing or dusting something.

Go to a well-known passage of Scripture and have a go at visualising it through the eyes of the writer. Write down your discoveries below.

## Reaction

My thoughts, notes and prayers

## Prayer

**Dear Father, I realise that meditation and memorising Your Word go hand in hand. Help me to be disciplined in these practices – for the sake of Your kingdom. Amen.**

## Memory Verse

Write down this week's verse and reference

## DAY 7 | Saturday

We are at the end of another week in our journey into learning to meditate in God's Word. I hope this past week has taught, blessed and challenged you as we have looked into the rewards of this discipline:

- True success. We saw this in the life of Joshua, that great warrior leader who succeeded Moses to lead Israel into the promised land. The crossing of the flood-swollen river Jordan, victory in many battles and the capture of many cities were all accomplished because Joshua had learned the value of spending time alone with God meditating on His Word.
- Understanding. In contrast to the world's knowledge and philosophies based on values mostly at variance and often diametrically opposed to God's eternal principles, Scripture meditation will gain us understanding beyond the comprehension of brilliant minds.
- A keener sense of the difference between right and wrong. God uses the Word hidden in our hearts through meditation to show us when our thoughts, attitudes and actions displease Him.
- Spiritual fruitfulness. Many Christians' lives are barren because they have never learned the joys of meditation. God promises us that those who meditate on His law will be like a tree bearing fruit and whose leaf never withers.
- Discovering how to live. Meditation helps to sharpen our minds, balance emotions and bring our wills more in line with His will.
- Biblical meditation helps us to absorb and memorise Scripture and we need to take practical steps to memorise more and more of His Word.

**Thought for today**

Biblical meditation brings the most lasting rewards.

## Action

Review the Re-establishing Your Priorities chart and Conclusion you filled in last week (pages 36–37) to see what improvements in the use of time you have made.

**READ JOHN 15:1-10**

Ponder on this passage, especially verses 7–8. How does it show the relationship between meditation and bearing much spiritual fruit? Write down your thoughts below.

## Reaction

My thoughts, notes and prayers

---

---

## Prayer

**Dear Lord, I want to be a Christian who bears more and more fruit for You. I realise that the key is meditating on Your Word. Amen.**

## More Exercises!

Write down these verses and memorise them: **Joshua 1:8; Psalm 119:11**

## A Goal to Aim For

The day may come when the Bible could be taken away from us – as has happened in some countries. So make it a goal to memorise a whole chapter of Scripture by a certain date. Don't make a vow to do this – just have a desire or goal. You never know what benefits your efforts will bring.

## Memory Verse

Write out this week's verse and reference

---

---

WEEK 4

# UNDERSTANDING WHAT BIBLICAL MEDITATION IS

WEEK 4

## DAY 1 | Sunday ______

# The Bible is unlike any other book

– it is the *living Word*. Time spent in the Scriptures changes us to be more like the Author: God Himself. He wants us to go into His Word expecting Him to speak to us and obeying what He says to us. This is the purpose of biblical meditation.

The Scriptures show us how to live according to His will and purposes, which is why His Word reveals Jesus as the only way to be reconciled to God. The Scriptures show us His absolutes for right and wrong – something that the greater majority of society ignores in pursuit of pleasure and material gain. Relativism holds sway in this age – no moral absolutes, anything goes. Christians, in contrast, are called to live in obedience to an unchanging God – which can only be done as we deeply absorb His Word and God speaks to our hearts through it.

**So, read this week's Memory Verse, write it down and spend time this Sabbath letting it challenge you:**

> *'How can a young man keep his way pure? By living according to your word.'*
> **PSALM 119:9**

______

______

______

To meditate on the Scriptures it will be helpful to understand exactly what meditation is and what it involves. This is the stage that we will cover this week in our journey of discovery. We will learn to 'chew the cud' of God's Word and then go on to see what a vast gulf there is between biblical meditation and other forms of meditation.

## DAY 2 | Monday

What exactly is biblical meditation? It is the process of holding a phrase or verse of Scripture in mind, pondering it, continually contemplating it, dwelling on it and viewing it from every angle we can think of until it begins to deeply affect us. Andrew Murray defined meditation as 'holding the Word of God in the mind until it has affected every area of one's life and character'.

Meditation has also been described by someone else as 'gazing long at a prism of many facets, turning it from angle to angle in a bright spotlight'. Bill Gothard likens meditation to a person slowly turning a many faceted diamond in the light to feast upon its beauty from every possible angle. Campbell McAlpine described it as 'the devotional practice of pondering the words of a verse, or verses of Scripture, with a receptive heart, allowing the Holy Spirit to take the written Word and apply it as a living word to the inner being'.

The word 'meditate' or 'meditation' can be found in many parts of the Bible. Psalm 1:2 tells of the person whose *'delight is in the law of the LORD, and on his law he meditates day and night.'* The Hebrew word for 'meditates' here is *hagah*, which means to murmur (in pleasure), to ponder.

Scripture meditation is the digestive system of the soul. The person who reads, studies and memorises the Bible without meditating on it is like one who chews their food but refuses to swallow it.

**Thought for today**

Contemplation of His Word is the springboard for living His life.

## Action

**READ PSALM 119:89-104**

What does this passage teach you about meditating on God's ways? In verse 99 the Hebrew word for 'meditate' here is *sichah* – to reflect with deep devotion. Ponder on the fact that meditation is the quiet contemplation and reflection on Scripture and write your thoughts below.

## Reaction

My thoughts, notes and prayers

## Prayer

**Father God, thank You that biblical meditation is a beautiful as well as an essential practice for me to learn and learn about. Amen.**

## Memory Verse

Write down this week's verse and reference

WEEK 4

# DAY 3 | Tuesday

In continuing to explore the meaning of meditation we come to another word to describe it: ruminate. Many animals – sheep, goats, camels, cows and giraffes – are known as ruminant animals because they have stomachs with several compartments, the first of which is called the rumen. The way a ruminant animal digests its food is quite fascinating. First it bolts its meal down, then later regurgitates the food out of its first stomach, the rumen, back into its mouth. This regurgitation process means the food is thoroughly digested, causing it to be absorbed into the bloodstream and become part of the animal's life.

Rumination and meditation are parallel words. When a Christian takes a thought from the Scriptures and begins to meditate on it they actually pass that thought from their mind into their spirit, backwards and forwards, over and over again, until it is absorbed into the spiritual bloodstream and translated into spiritual faith and energy.

Just as a ruminant animal gets its nourishment and energy from the grass through regurgitation so does a Christian extract from the Scriptures the life of Christ through meditation. Meditation on the Word of God transfers the life of Christ into the believer's personality. So remember: it is not enough simply to read the Bible, study the Bible or memorise the Bible. To extract the life of God that He has deposited in it we must meditate upon it.

**Thought for today**

I must chew on God's
Word to be fully fed.

## Action

**READ JOHN 15:1-16.**

Ponder verse 5: *'It is the man who shares my life and whose life I share who proves fruitful'*, using J.B. Phillips' version, if you have it. Do another word study about the meaning of meditation by turning to **Psalm 19:14**. The word for 'meditation' here is *higgayon*, meaning a musical notation, a murmuring sound. Meditation is a musical repetition of God's Word. Write down your thoughts and prayers below.

## Reaction

My thoughts, notes and prayers

---

---

---

## Prayer

**Dear Lord, I see that I must chew on Your Word, so that Your life may flow in me. I am so grateful to know this. Amen.**

## Memory Verse

Write out this week's verse and reference

---

---

---

# DAY 4 | Wednesday

Reading, studying and memorising the Bible are primarily intellectual exercises that bring spiritual results. Meditation, however, is not primarily an intellectual exercise but a way by which the Word of God is carried direct into the human spirit where it can accomplish its greatest work.

To understand what goes on in meditation we must see the difference between the soul and the spirit. The Bible teaches that there are three parts to our being: spirit, soul and body (1 Thess. 5:23). The spirit is the centre of our personality, the motivating part of our whole being. The Scriptures also teach that there is a clear difference between the spirit and the soul (Heb. 4:12; Luke 1:46–47). The spirit is the centre of our personality – what the Bible sometimes speaks of as the 'heart'. The soul is that part of us which contains our mind (or thoughts), feelings and decisions. When we read, study or memorise the Bible the action goes on in our minds and eventually passes into our spirits. But when we meditate we drop the Word of God instantly into our spirits so that it can achieve maximum effectiveness.

To come back to that word 'ruminate', biblical meditation is all about passing His Word from the soul to the spirit – backwards and forwards, over and over again – so it can do its cleansing, healing, transforming work. To get the best out of life great matters have to be given a second thought. Biblical meditation is just that: giving Scriptural truths a second thought.

### Thought for today

How can I ignore giving God's truths a second thought!

## Action

**READ PSALM 4:1-8**

Especially ponder verse 4 (AV rendering): '*... commune with your own heart upon your bed, and be still.*' Write down below what it says to you about meditation. Also turn to **1 Timothy 4:15** (AV). The word translated 'meditate' here is *meletao* – to ponder carefully with the mind, to muse upon. Meditation is a careful and prayerful reviewing of Scripture.

## Reaction

My thoughts, notes and prayers

## Prayer

**Father God, anoint my eyes to see the truth I am looking at, for I know only too well that the natural mind cannot understand the things of God because they can only be spiritually discerned. Thank You. Amen.**

## Memory Verse

Write down this week's verse and reference

## DAY 5 | Thursday

So much depends on a clear understanding of the meaning of biblical meditation. As we have seen, it is the spiritual exercise we go through when we hold a word, a thought or a verse of Scripture in our minds before dropping it into our spirits, bringing it back again into the mind, returning it to the spirit, backwards and forwards, over and over again, until we extract from it the very life of Christ that lies in His Word. Just as a cow chews the cud we gain every ounce of nourishment from the Word of God as we pass it from our mind to our spirit until we have thoroughly digested it spiritually.

It cannot be emphasised enough that biblical meditation is the only beneficial type of meditation because it focuses on God's thoughts – not our own. Avoid getting alone with your own thoughts because it is dangerous to rummage around in thoughts of the past – mistakes you made, how romances might have turned out, examination flops ... Put these thoughts behind you once and for all and concentrate on thinking God's thoughts.

Once you have grasped the concept of meditation and know how to apply it to your life you will find your spirit becoming the secret workshop of an unseen Sculptor chiselling in the secret chambers of your heart, the living forms that contribute to your character development. Through this your life will be a radiant testimony to the power and grace of the Lord Jesus Christ.

### Thought for today

Thinking God's thoughts brings no regrets.

## Action

**READ PROVERBS 4:14-27**

Write down below what God is saying to you through this passage. Consider what areas of your heart especially need to be guarded (verse 23).

## Reaction

My thoughts, notes and prayers

______________________________________________

______________________________________________

______________________________________________

## Prayer

**Dear Lord, help me from now on to focus more on Your thoughts than I do on my own. Amen.**

## Memory Verse

Write down this week's verse and reference

______________________________________________

______________________________________________

______________________________________________

## DAY 6 | Friday

# There are many forms

of meditation being practised today – the most popular being transcendental meditation (TM). Made popular by an Indian mystic, Maharishi Mahesh Yogi, TM is expanding rapidly in Western society. Yogi claims that TM 'is a form of prayer and a path to God'. He believes that by stilling the mind and stopping all perception and thought one merges with the universe and experiences 'transcendence' by making contact with God, who is described as the impersonal 'All'.

More words of Maharishi Mahesh Yogi show at once how the whole TM system is totally at odds with God's revelation of Himself in the Scriptures: *'The practice of transcendental meditation unfolds the full potential of the divine in man and brings human consciousness to the level of God consciousness ... A most refined and powerful form of prayer is this meditation, which leads us to the field of the Creator, to the sources of Creation, to the field of God.'*

The experience of 'transcendence', of being lifted up to God, is illusory and unbiblical. If putting one's thoughts into neutral enables a person to climb up to God then the incarnation of Jesus was unnecessary. In seeking to help people get to know God, TM bypasses Jesus Christ and any system of religion seeking to do that is anti-Christ. According to TM, a person has the answer to their own destiny within themselves. It fails to recognise that our human nature has a bias that will lead us away from God rather than toward Him.

### Thought for today

God is the Master of my destiny – not me.

## Action

**READ ROMANS 3:21-26**

Write below the main differences between biblical meditation and transcendental meditation, especially in the light of verse 23 of the passage.

## Reaction

My thoughts, notes and prayers

## Prayer

**I am so glad, Heavenly Father, that I cannot climb up to You, but You came down to me through sending Jesus to be the Saviour of the world. Amen.**

## Memory Verse

Write down this week's verse and reference

# DAY 7 | Saturday

As we come to the end of this week we realise that we have been gaining an understanding of what exactly biblical meditation is and what it involves. We have also been seeing what it is not – especially that there is an unbridgeable gulf between biblical meditation and other forms of meditation.

- Biblical meditation involves dwelling on a passage, verse or phrase of Scripture, continually thinking about it, tossing it up and down, looking at it from every angle. It is mulling over Scripture, deeply absorbing it so that it affects our thoughts and actions.
- The process of meditation can be described as 'chewing the cud' – an expression that comes from the way animals such as cows, goats and sheep bolt down food, regurgitate it back into their mouths and repeat the process over and over again until it is absorbed into the bloodstream and becomes part of their life. Biblical meditation does this in a spiritual sense to a Christian's life – taking something from the Scriptures and passing it backwards and forwards between their mind and spirit until it becomes part of their spiritual bloodstream.
- Biblical meditation is the process through which God transfers the life of Christ into the Christian's personality.
- Transcendental meditation is at odds with biblical meditation because it advocates putting one's thoughts into neutral to be able to climb up to God. If one was able to do that then the incarnation of Jesus – God come down to us – was unnecessary.

**Thought for today**

There is no type of meditation that compares with biblical meditation.

## SOME OF THE DIFFERENCES BETWEEN TRANSCENDENTAL AND BIBLICAL MEDITATION

### TRANSCENDENTAL MEDITATION

- Seeks to empty the mind of all activity and thought.
- Can open the personality to unknown spiritual forces.
- Focuses on bringing man to God.
- Encourages a belief in self-dependency.
- Says that man's greatest sin is that he is ignorant of being divine.
- Believes that man can overcome sin by meditation.
- Says the answer to every problem is there is no problem.
- Involves worship of a *deceased guru* – Guru Dev.
- Recognises a number of gods using the mantra.
- Claims that the key to fulfilment of every religion is found in the regular practice of TM.

### BIBLICAL MEDITATION

- Seeks to fill the mind with thoughts of God (Matt. 22:37).
- Teaches man to be alert to the activity of evil spiritual forces (Eph. 6:12)
- Focus on how God comes to man (Col. 2:9).
- Encourages a belief in God-dependency (John 15:5).
- Proclaims that the way to God is through Christ alone (John 14:6).
- Focuses on the blood of Christ for the expiation of sin (1 John 1:7).
- Encourages a dependence on Christ for spiritual strength (Matt. 11:28).
- Concentrates on one living God (Acts 2:32).
- Declares one God, in the first biblical commandment (Exod. 20:3).
- Affirms that there is one mediator between God and man – Jesus Christ (1 Tim. 2:5).

# DAY 7 | Saturday

## Action

| Try this test | TRUE | FALSE |
|---|---|---|
| **1.** Biblical meditation is actively putting the mind into a state of relaxation. | ☐ | ☐ |
| **2.** Biblical meditation begins when we turn our thoughts towards God. | ☐ | ☐ |
| **3.** A guaranteed way of getting a peaceful night's sleep is to meditate on God's Word. | ☐ | ☐ |
| **4.** Biblical meditation enhances the study of the Bible by ensuring that the Word becomes 'flesh'– in us. | ☐ | ☐ |
| **5.** A major difference between Transcendental Meditation and biblical meditation is that TM focuses on emptying the mind while biblical meditation focuses on filling it with the Word of God. | ☐ | ☐ |
| **6.** Biblical meditation helps a person develop dependency on their own inner resources. | ☐ | ☐ |

| | TRUE | FALSE |
|---|---|---|
| **7.** Biblical meditation assists a person in developing spiritual sensitivity and awareness. | ☐ | ☐ |
| **8.** A good way to learn to begin the art of biblical meditation is to memorise a whole chapter and then focus on it verse by verse. | ☐ | ☐ |
| **9.** The Bible says there are three key periods in a day when we can meditate. | ☐ | ☐ |

**Answers to this test can be found on page 99**

WEEK 5

# HOW TO MEDITATE

# DAY 1 | Sunday

**Memories.** We all have them, good and bad, depending on our experiences of life. Some things we recall with pleasure and pride: academic achievements, scoring the winning goal for your team, dating the girl or man we are now married to, children, grandchildren ... There may be other things we'd rather not remember, at any rate in too much detail: bad childhood experiences, a failed romance, financial troubles, horrific experiences in war ... Most of us easily remember the good and important things in our lives and consign the unimportant and negative into the deep recesses of our memories where they are more easily forgotten. For the Christian there is one thing above all else that God wants us to fix firmly in our memories and to recall throughout each day: His Word.

Over the next few days we will be learning how to meditate and start putting this into practice. We will begin by learning to understand the true meaning of Scripture in its context before moving on to the practising of memorising every word of the text being meditated on, the significance of key words, using Scripture in prayer, applying it to our lives and, finally, letting it minister to us whether we are awake or asleep.

**In your quiet time today mull over each word of this text one at a time and then read it slowly, putting emphasis on what you feel are the key words. Let the Holy Spirit use the scripture to draw out praise to God.**

> *'Therefore, if anyone is in Christ, he is a new creation; the old has gone, the new has come!'*
> **2 CORINTHIANS 5:17**

(NB There will be no Memory Verse from this week to allow us to focus on the application of the art of biblical meditation.)

# DAY 2 | Monday

Now that you have a grasp of why biblical meditation is so important for a Christian we are turning to the nitty-gritty: *how* to do it. First, select an appropriate verse or passage of Scripture. Newcomers to meditation will most probably find it more helpful to start by meditating on one phrase or text rather than a long passage or chapter. Pick a text that tugs at your heart and seems as if it is saying, 'Please meditate on me!' For example:

> *'Man does not live on bread alone, but on every word that comes from the mouth of God.'* **MATTHEW 4:4**

Secondly, seek to understand the true meaning of the verse in its context. It has been said that 'a verse taken out of its context becomes a pretext'. It is possible to remove a scripture out of its biblical setting and make it mean something entirely different. The verse chosen is taken from the account of Christ's temptation in the wilderness. Our Lord was making the point that it was more important to live by the words of God than to satisfy His physical hunger. Make sure that you understand the meaning of every word in the text. A dictionary, Bible dictionary or Bible commentary will help. You may like to find out something about the cultural backcloth to the text – the Eastern customs and practices of the day and so on. This will enrich your understanding and encourage you to know more of God through His Word.

**Thought for today**

God's Word is the most valuable thing to remember.

## Action

**READ MATTHEW 4:1-11**

Make some notes below about the setting of this passage, the significance of Jesus' statement in verse 4. You could consider things such as how (physically) hungry our Lord was, the effects of the desert heat, what the devil was offering Him, the consequences if He had accepted the devil's offer, why Jesus rejected it and how His response speaks to us about Christian commitment.

## Reaction

My thoughts, notes and prayers

## Prayer

**Dear Lord, help me to make more and more of Your Word real in my life. For the sake of Your kingdom. Amen.**

# DAY 3 | Tuesday

Another key to fruitful biblical meditation is to memorise every word of the text you wish to meditate on. Those who reckon they have a bad memory and have trouble in recalling anything are usually people who have not learned the simple principles of memorisation. Study and practise these three basic principles:

1. Read the phrase or text slowly so that every word sinks in. Do this several times – out loud if you can. Our ears are a vital part of our memory.
2. Underline the key words. For example: '**Man** does not **live** on **bread** alone **but** on every **word** that comes out of the **mouth** of **God**.' Now repeat the verse several times emphasising the words in bold type.
3. Write out the verse several times. This is a tip many have found useful when attempting to memorise a passage of Scripture. Write it out a dozen times and the chances are you will never forget it.

Visualise as far as you are able the significance of each and every key word. For example: '**Man**' – all mankind, every person. This is a universal principle. Everyone is included. 'Man **does not**' – a final decree. No one will change it. It is a definite negate. 'Man does not **live**' – living is more than existing. There is a physical life and a spiritual life. God made us to enjoy the pleasures of life in a relationship with Him.

**Thought for today**

Repeating God's Word to myself is far from boring repetition.

## Action

**READ JOHN 3:16-21**

Choose a verse or phrase from it and apply the principles you have just been reading about to help you memorise it. Write down your thoughts below.

## Reaction

My thoughts, notes and prayers

## Prayer

**Heavenly Father, please increase my ability to memorise the Scriptures so that You, working through them, can transform me. Amen.**

# DAY 4 | Wednesday

In learning how to meditate on God's Word it is important to let a verse, phrase or passage go out of your consciousness and then bring it back. This should be done as often as you can. This action not only helps to impress the Bible text more deeply upon your spirit but will give you practice in retrieving it from your memory – recalling it. There will be times when you urgently need to reach for a text – in witnessing about Christ to someone, for example, or when you suddenly experience fierce temptation. The more practice you have of hiding a text in your memory and retrieving it the more effective your spiritual life will be.

It's also vital to use Scripture as a talking point with God. Using Matthew 4:4 again as a sample text you could pray something like:

> *'O Lord, I am so grateful that you have given me Your Word which, as Job said, is more important than my daily meals. Help me to see that, just as I am dependent upon physical nourishment to get through the day, I also have to depend on Your Word for the spiritual sustenance I need to meet the challenges of life.'*

In this way you are not only deepening your understanding of a text but adding a new dimension to your prayer life.

**Thought for today**

Scripture is the best talking point.

## Action

**READ PSALM 23**

Choose a verse, phrase – or even the whole Psalm if you wish – and practise letting it go out of your consciousness and back again. Use it to talk to God. Write down your thoughts below.

## Reaction

My thoughts, notes and prayers

## Prayer

**Dear Lord, thank You for showing me that using Scripture in prayer is a wonderful way of talking with You. Amen.**

# DAY 5 | Thursday

Now we come to an all-important issue: how to apply what we are meditating upon to our life. Bible meditation and memorising verses, phrases and passages of the Scriptures would be a waste of time unless we let God change us through it. He not only wants us to be hearers of His Word but doers of it! I repeat: We must allow His Word to change us.

Those who have long practised meditation say that the more they personalised a verse of Scripture the more impact it had upon them. Let's use Matthew 4:4 again as an example:

'Man does not **live** ...' I don't just want to be alive – I want to live, really live. This means that I must let God live His life through me. I must consider how I let Him see through my eyes, speak through my lips, love through my heart and work through my hands.

' ... on bread **alone** ...' If I am to have God's life I must make sure I pay more attention to my spiritual diet than my physical diet. Food is important but God's Word is even more important. I need more of it!

' ... but on every **word** ...' *Every* word? If every word is so important to my spiritual health how many do I know? I wish I had started meditating on God's Word before now, but better late than never. I must make it a top priority to get to know the Scriptures better!

### Thought for today

God's Word is food for action.

## Action

**READ HEBREWS 12:1-13**

What is God saying personally to you through this passage – or a particular part of it? Write down your thoughts below.

## Reaction

My thoughts, notes and prayers

## Prayer

**Heavenly Father, I want Your Word to change me – more and more. Amen.**

# DAY 6 | Friday

Another key to effective meditation is quoting a verse of Scripture to ourselves just before we go to sleep and again as we wake up. I touched on this in The Purposes of Biblical Meditation (Week 2), but it is equally important to emphasise here. The last thought on your mind before you go to sleep will drop down in your subconscious and be active during the night hours.

Every night as we go to sleep a marvellous transition takes place. The conscious mind hands over to the subconscious mind the responsibility of keeping everything under control. The task of the subconscious mind is to rebuild the physical and mental parts of the body so that they are ready to begin another day. It does so by decelerating the heartbeat from 72 beats per minute to 60 or less. If all goes to plan we wake up the next morning refreshed and ready for the day ahead.

But if the conscious mind transfers a deep or pressing problem to the subconscious a restless night might well result. The subconscious mind doesn't want to handle fears and negative thoughts because they interfere with rejuvenating the system. But if the subconscious mind is handed a part of God's Word it delights in it, for this is what it was made for. So get into the habit of going to sleep with God's Word in your mind and on your lips so He can work in you during your slumbering hours.

## Thought for today

I will let God have the last word at night and the first word in the morning.

## Action

**READ PROVERBS 2:1-11**

Memorise a verse or phrase from this passage and quote it just before you go to sleep tonight and as soon as you wake up in the morning. You may prefer, of course, to try it with Matthew 4:4, 2 Corinthians 5:17 or another text.

## Reaction

My thoughts, notes and prayers

______________________________

______________________________

______________________________

______________________________

## Prayer

**Heavenly Father, I want Your Word to be on my mind and in my heart when I am awake and when I am asleep. Please help it to be so. Amen.**

# DAY 7 | Saturday

This week we have really got down to the business of meditating, a key part of which is memorising Scripture. Those new to meditation were encouraged to begin with a phrase or short verse, such as Matthew 4:4. You were encouraged to seek to understand a text like this in its context, for seeing Scripture in its biblical setting is so important. Then we moved on to:

- getting into the habit of memorising every word of the text we meditate upon, taking simple steps to help remember texts.
- the importance of letting Scripture go out of the consciousness, bringing it back to mind and repeating the process as often as possible to help it go more deeply into our spirits.
- personalising passages of Scripture so that God can work powerfully in our lives. Every word is important, so it is vital that we get to know more and more of it.
- quoting a verse of Scripture as we go to sleep and as soon as we wake up, allowing His Word to do His work in us through our slumbering hours.

One result of learning to meditate is that God's Word is engrafted into our heart to produce spiritual qualities and characteristics that enrich our personality – just as in horticulture it is possible to take a shoot, bud or branch and graft it on to an established plant or tree to bear new fruit or flowers. As we continually meditate on Scripture God's truth becomes a part of our life.

**Thought for today**

Scripture is God's tool to work in my life.

## Action

Set out below are the key points that we have covered over the last two weeks as we have worked towards the actual practice of biblical meditation. As you go through next week use this list to help ensure that you are applying each of the techniques we have covered. You may like to copy these key points on to a piece of card to use as a bookmark.

### DESCRIPTIONS OF BIBLICAL MEDITATION (FROM WEEK 4)

1. Slowly turning a many faceted diamond in the light to feast upon its beauty from every angle.
2. Rumination. Rumination and meditation are parallel words. As a ruminant animal gets nourishment from rumination so does a Christian extract the life of Christ through biblical meditation.

### KEYS TO THE PRACTICE OF BIBLICAL MEDITATION (FROM WEEK 5)

1. (Day 2). Select verses which 'speak' to you.
2. (Day 2). Seek understanding of true meaning of the text in its context.
3. (Day 2). Understand every word in the text. Use a Bible dictionary or commentary.
4. (Day 3). Memorise every word of the text using these principles:
   - read slowly out loud
   - underline key words
   - write out several times
   - visualise significance of each key word.
5. (Day 4). Let the text go in and out of your consciousness.
6. (Day 4). Use the text as a talking point with God.
7. (Day 5). Allow God's Word to change you.
8. (Day 6). Quote text to yourself before going to sleep.

WEEK 5

# DAY 7 | Saturday ______________________

## THE FOLLOWING ASSIGNMENT WILL HELP YOU APPLY THE TECHNIQUES WE HAVE LEARNED.

Use this style of form to help you get the best from each **Meditation Verse** over the next week.

**MEDITATE ON ROMANS 8:38-39**

1. FOR I AM CONVINCED THAT NEITHER DEATH NOR LIFE ...
(Thoughts and comments)

______________________________

______________________________

2. NEITHER ANGELS NOR DEMONS ...

______________________________

______________________________

3. NEITHER THE PRESENT NOR THE FUTURE ...

______________________________

______________________________

4. NOR ANY POWERS ...

______________________________

______________________________

5. NEITHER HEIGHT NOR DEPTH ...

______________________________

______________________________

6. NOR ANYTHING ELSE IN ALL CREATION ...

7. WILL BE ABLE TO SEPARATE US ...

8. FROM THE LOVE OF GOD THAT IS IN CHRIST JESUS OUR LORD.

## Reaction

My thoughts, notes and prayers

## Prayer

**Lord, thank You for all that You are teaching me about the importance and practice of biblical meditation. I am so grateful that You are changing me through it. Amen.**

### Thought for Today

The abiding presence of the Holy Spirit enables us to understand Scripture as God meant it.

WEEK 6

# FROM THEORY TO PRACTICE

WEEK 6

# DAY 1 | Sunday

We have been seeing that through meditation we can engraft the Word of God into our life and bring about major changes in our personality. Over the last week of our journey together we will focus on the application of biblical meditation to make us more like Jesus. There are nine qualities we need to concentrate on to develop Christ-likeness, all of them in Galatians 5:22–23. John Stott wrote in *Essentials for Tomorrow's Christians*: 'I long to see our evangelical faith exhibiting the fruit of the Spirit,' adding that for many years he had daily recited the nine-fold fruit of the Spirit in the above verses to himself and prayed for the fulness of the Spirit.

This week we will be looking at and learning to apply through meditation three of the fruit of the Spirit: love, joy and peace. We will spend two days on each fruit and a Scripture verse is given for meditation over each two-day period to help you begin, through yielding to the Spirit, to make these attributes part of your life.

In the previous five weeks Day 7 has been used to help you review what you have learned since the start of that particular week. Through this I hope that you have learned the importance of constant review in meditating on the Scriptures – enough to invite you to write your own review at the end of this week. The set Prayer section, which has been a regular feature in our studies, ceased at the end of Week 5 because prayers of your own should become a natural consequence of your meditations.

**To set the scene for the coming week read Galatians 5:22–23 and meditate on the fruit of the Spirit so vital to Christian life and witness.**

# DAY 2 | Monday

We Christians need the fulness of the Holy Spirit to reveal the fruit of the Spirit in our lives. Are you *filled* with the Spirit? Having the Spirit within results in a quality of life with nine characteristics, the first of which is love. This emphasis on love being foremost fits in with the apostle Paul's emphasis in 1 Corinthians chapter 13. Love is the outcome of the Spirit within and if this is lacking everything is lacking.

Make it your goal today to meditate on this priceless passage of Scripture. Do what many Christians do when meditating upon verses 4–7: substitute your name for the word *love*. How does it sound now? If we want to become more like Jesus then we must grow in love, for without love we are nothing.

You may be tempted to protest that in *your* situation it isn't easy to love. Things may be difficult at work or there's a deep relationship problem in the family. But that's the kind of environment the Holy Spirit thrives upon to make you more and more like Jesus. A newly-arrived missionary was treated roughly by the one she was responsible to. The older woman was spiritually dry, hardened through years of labour without seeing much fruit. That young lady faced the problem by daily going to 1 Corinthians 13 *on her knees* until eventually her older colleague broke down before her in tears and confessed her wrong attitudes. God's love conquers all!

**Thought for today**

God's love within me breaks through the impossible.

## Action

Our **Meditation Verses** for today and tomorrow are:

**1 CORINTHIANS 13:4-7**

> *'Love is patient, love is kind. It does not envy, it does not boast, it is not proud. It is not rude, it is not self-seeking, it is not easily angered, it keeps no record of wrongs. Love does not delight in evil but rejoices with the truth. It always protects, always trusts, always hopes, always perseveres.'*

Write down the verses for yourself on a meditation card and meditate on them using the practical steps learned last week. Keep your meditation card with you for constant reference through the day.

To help your meditations substitute your name for *love* in these verses. Think about Paul's life and how he displayed Christ-like love in many hostile situations – see **2 Corinthians 4:7-11**, for example.

Write down what God is saying to you below.

## Reaction

My thoughts, notes and prayers

---

---

---

---

---

WEEK 6

# DAY 3 | Tuesday

How mature are you as a Christian? You might answer this question by saying that you have known Jesus Christ as your personal Saviour for a good number of years. But knowledge in itself does not produce spiritual maturity, as 1 Corinthians 8:1 tells us. J.B. Phillips translates this verse as: '... while knowledge may make a man look big, it is only love that can make him grow to his full stature.' Biblical meditation can help us to be more Christ-like in character – to love as He loves.

The love a Christian has must be different from any other kind of love – the love of Christ. Paul the apostle was able to declare that he was controlled by this love. A lot of people are controlled by the love of success, of achievement and, most of all, money. What kind of love controls you? Is it the love of a cause or the love of Christ?

God's desire is for His Son's love to flow in and through us like water. When water moves over an incline and strikes a wheel it creates power. If it touches a plant it gives life. Does Christ's love flow into your life enough to impact the people you meet who need their lives transformed by Him? Meditate on 1 Corinthians 8:1 again and ask yourself: Am I someone who merely has a good deal of knowledge or someone who knows how to love with Christ's love?

**Thought for Today**

Christ's love in me is the language of God's heart.

## Action

Continue your meditations on **1 Corinthians 13:4-7** using the steps we have learned.

Ask yourself: Is there anything I do and say that is causing problems with my fellow brothers and sisters in Christ? What changes do I need to make so that Christ's love can flow through me to encourage them? Write your response below.

Remind yourself of the keys to biblical meditation in Week 5 Day 7.

## Reaction

My thoughts, notes and prayers

---

---

---

---

---

# DAY 4 | Wednesday ______________

Are you a joyful Christian? Do unbelievers see an exuberance in you that defies logic? Joy is a fruit of the Holy Spirit and follows love, for it is a by-product of love. Joy should be the main characteristic of every Christian, but many know little or nothing of it. They are under the lash of duty rather than under the control of an inner light – the Spirit. Some not only don't expect joy – they don't want it either. Life, for them, has to be lived seriously, solemnly, but a faith with roots in an Easter morning must express itself in abounding joy. We were made for joy, not gloom. The empty tomb takes away our empty gloom. To a Christian joy is inevitable. If there is no joy there is something wrong.

**This is why our Meditation Verses for today and tomorrow are:**

> *'Be joyful always; pray continually; give thanks in all circumstances, for this is God's will for you in Christ Jesus.*
> **1 THESSALONIANS 5:16-18**

Note that it says 'always'. To thank God for everything means that we must see God in everything. In times of gloom and sadness we must look the trouble in the eye and say something like: 'If God has allowed you to come then it can only help me, not hurt me. So I will do what the psalmist did – make a joyful noise to the rock of our salvation.' If you do this you will get a joyful echo from that Rock in return.

---

## Thought for today

The empty tomb has dealt joyfully with my gloom.

## Action

**READ 1 THESSALONIANS 5:4-24**

Write out and memorise the **Meditation Verses:** 16–18.

Consider all the reasons here for being joyful. Meditate on the **Meditation Verses** considering the part that prayer has in meditation.

Note what you have learned below.

## Reaction

My thoughts, notes and prayers

## DAY 5 | Thursday

# We cannot absorb Christ's joy without it affecting our own joy. 'I have told you this, that my joy may be within you and your joy complete,' says Moffatt's translation of John 15:11. Our Lord's joy completes our joy. The idea that Christians will one day discover that joy in heaven instead of having a joy that supports us while we are still on earth is false. Some Christians may be heading for glory but there's nothing of being on the glory road about them right now!

Let's look at some more Moffatt translations of Scripture about joy. '*... let us enjoy the peace we have with God*' (Rom. 5:1). Some have peace with God but don't enjoy it. ' *... we enjoy our redemption*' (Eph. 1:7). To be redeemed and not enjoy it is a contradiction in terms. ' *... we ... enjoy our access to the Father in one Spirit*' (Eph. 2:18). ' *... we enjoy our confidence of free access*' (Eph. 3:12). These scriptures show us that joy is overflowing because of peace, redemption and access to the Father. Your situation may be dark and dismal but if you meditate on the fact that God is your heavenly Father, Jesus is your Saviour, the angels are your companions, heaven is your home and you have free access to the throne of God I guarantee that joy will spring up in you. It must. Joy to a Christian is a necessity – not a luxury.

### Thought for today

Joy is for now

- not just for eternity.

## Action

Remind yourself of the keys to biblical meditation, read **John 15:5-17** and use what these verses say about the conditions for being able to experience complete joy to help you meditate again on the **Meditation Verses.** Read and reflect again on the **Meditation Verses** before you go to sleep tonight.

## Reaction

My thoughts, notes and prayers

_______________________________________________

_______________________________________________

_______________________________________________

_______________________________________________

_______________________________________________

# DAY 6 | Friday

Peace. It's something most people want above all. Peace in their homes, in their families, in their work situations. Peace in their minds. Peace is the third quality of the Spirit and Christians must possess it in order to become Christ-like in character. This is more than peace of mind: it is peace of spirit. A woman once told me, 'I turned to religion [note: religion, not Christ] to obtain peace of mind. Although it helped me greatly it couldn't compare with the experience I discovered in transcendental meditation.' The fact that she was looking for peace of mind showed the shallowness of her quest.

You cannot have peace of mind unless you have something deeper – the peace of God. It is a peace that begins in the spirit. Peace of mind is the outcome of the deeper peace in the spirit. You cannot have peace of mind if there is conflict in the spirit. As one preacher put it, 'To know the peace of God you must know the God of peace.' To tinker with the mind and leave the depths untouched is unproductive. It only produces a peace that goes to pieces.

True peace comes from adjustment to reality, which can only come from adjustment to God. Peace of mind breaks down if the worm of doubt is eating at its centre. When calamity comes peace is shattered. Christian peace flows out of a right personal relationship with God and His Son the Lord Jesus Christ.

**This is why our Meditation Verse for today and tomorrow is:**

> *'Peace I leave with you; my peace I give you. I do not give to you as the world gives. Do not let your hearts be troubled and do not be afraid.'*
> **JOHN 14:27**

## Thought for today

Only God's peace
is real peace.

## Action

**READ JOHN 14:12-27.**

Write down and memorise the **Meditation Verse – John 14:27.**

Do you have the peace this passage reveals Christians should have – the true peace of God? What are conditions for knowing God's peace? Look at **Philippians 4:4-7**. What do these verses say about the quality of peace God gives? Do you really have it? What is God saying to you about His peace? Bear this in mind as you meditate today on the new **Meditation Verse**.

Write down your thoughts and responses below.

## Reaction

My thoughts, notes and prayers

# DAY 7 | Saturday

Although true peace begins in a right relationship with God there must be a conscious centring of the mind on Him for this peace to continue. It is no use treating God as one to occasionally refer to – He must be the centre of our affections and loyalty. More than that, He must be the centre of our trust. W.B. Yeats describes what happens to those who do not trust in God:

> *Things fall apart; the centre cannot hold.*
> *Mere anarchy is loosed upon the world ...*
> *The best lacks all conviction, while the worst*
> *Are full of passionate intensity.*

The 'centre cannot hold' if it is not rooted in God. People fall into the trap of thinking that accumulation of wealth and possessions will stave off anxiety. Instead they find anxiety increases.

Someone told me that his wife had a disease called 'gadgetitis'. I was puzzled until he explained that whenever she got a gadget she became unhappy because she wondered how long it would be before another gadget made the current one obsolete. She also worried about being able to afford the new one when it came out. The cure for this and other 'ills' is for God alone to be the centre of our affections on an ongoing basis. Then we will know His peace continually. Focus on His promise today: *'You will keep in perfect peace him whose mind is steadfast, because he trusts in you.'*

---

**Thought for today**

Affection for God is central to my peace.

## Action

**READ ISAIAH 26:1-12**

What are the reasons here for trusting God? How do they relate to ongoing peace in a believer's heart? How does this passage relate to my circumstances and God's calling on my life?

Remind yourself again of the keys to meditation. Continue to meditate on the **Meditation Verse.**

Review what you have learned through your Bible meditations this week.

Write down your answers, thoughts and response to God below.

## Reaction

My thoughts, notes and prayers

# THE FINAL WORD

## Our secret meditations become us – for good or ill.

It is now time to summarise what we have been saying over these past six weeks. We have seen that to read, study, memorise and even analyse the Bible is not enough – to get the best out of it we must spend time meditating upon it. If we are to grow in Christ-likeness then we must learn that what we hold in our minds passes automatically into our emotions and from there affects our decisions and ultimately our actions.

Thoughts are powerful – they are not passive things. If, for example, we allow our imagination to dwell upon things that are impure and forbidden by God then it will not be long before the thought turns into action. What we take into our minds in meditation will stay in our lives as fact. We must hold nothing in our minds that we do not want to hold within us permanently. The power of meditation is tremendous and as we learn to harness this power to the Word of God, use it daily to reconstruct our thought life, refocus our emotions and realign our wills, it will not be long before others begin to see the characteristics of the Lord Jesus Christ appearing in us. The Living Word is revealed to us through the power of the written Word, held and meditated upon in our minds. Whatever else you might forget from these studies, remember this:

**What you put into your mind today as meditation will come out tomorrow as fact.**

**Answers to Test - Week 4 Day 7.**

1. False. Meditation is an activity – engaging the mind and spirit with the content of God's eternal Word.
2. False. Meditation is not thinking our thoughts about God but thinking His thoughts after Him.
3. False. Meditation may help us to sleep peacefully but at first it may dislodge impure thoughts which are entrenched in our minds. This can cause unpleasant dreams which may continue until our minds are purified by the Word of God.
4. True.
5. True.
6. False. The more we meditate on God's Word the more we will come to see the importance of depending upon God rather than upon our own strength and ideas.
7. True.
8. False. Beginners should start with a single text not a whole chapter. You cannot learn to run until you have learned to walk.
9. False. It says there are four (see Deut. 6:7).

## Help young people experience God and grow as followers of Jesus

**PENS**

These 30 days of undated, daily Bible-reading notes featuring the Pens characters are ideal for adults to use with 3- to 6-year-olds to help them enjoy daily Bible reading and develop a love for God's Word.
Price: £3.99 each per single issue

**TOPZ**

The Topz Gang teach children aged 7-11 biblical truths through bimonthly dated, daily Bible readings, cartoons, prayers, word games, puzzles and competitions.
Price: £2.75 each
One-year subscription (UK) 6 issues: £14.95

**YP's**

Encourages 11- to 15-year-olds to dig deeper into God's Word through bimonthly dated, daily Bible readings, with reviews, interviews and competitions.
Price: £2.75 each
One-year subscription (UK) 6 issues: £14.95

**METTLE**

This contemporary four-monthly daily, dated devotional for 14- to 18-year-olds is jointly produced by CWR and Youth for Christ.
Price: £4.75 each
One-year subscription (UK) 3 issues: £13.80

## Know God better and be strengthened spiritually

Our compact, daily Bible-reading notes for adults are published bimonthly and offer a focus for every need. They are available as individual issues or annual subscriptions, in print or by email.
**One-year subscription (UK): £14.95**
**Single issue: £2.75**

### EVERY DAY WITH JESUS

With around a million readers, this insightful devotional by Selwyn Hughes is one of the most popular daily Bible-reading tools in the world. A large-print edition is also available.
72-page booklets, 120x170mm
ISSN: 0967-1889
Large Print edition: ISSN: 0967-4381, 210x197mm

### INSPIRING WOMEN EVERY DAY

Written by women, for women, to inspire, encourage and strengthen.
64-page booklets, 120x170mm
ISSN: 1478-050 X

### LUCAS ON LIFE EVERY DAY

Apply the Bible to life each day with these challenging life-application notes written by international speaker and well-known author Jeff Lucas.
64-page booklets, 120x170mm
ISSN: 1744-0122

### COVER TO COVER EVERY DAY

Study one Old Testament and one New Testament book in depth with each issue, and a psalm every weekend. Two well-known Bible scholars each contribute a month's series of daily Bible studies. Covers every book of the Bible in five years.
64-page booklets, 120x170mm
ISSN: 1744-0114

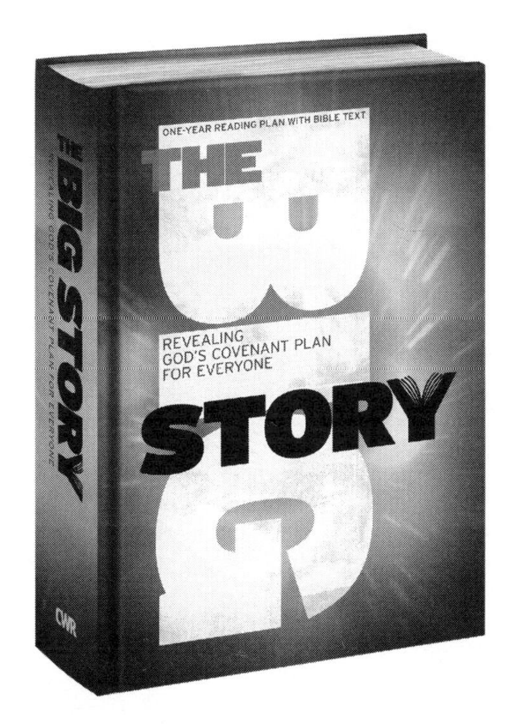
ONE-YEAR READING PLAN WITH BIBLE TEXT
THE
BIG
STORY
REVEALING
GOD'S COVENANT PLAN
FOR EVERYONE
THE BIG STORY
REVEALING GOD'S COVENANT PLAN FOR EVERYONE
CWR

## Journey through the Bible in a year of daily readings with insightful commentary

*Cover to Cover Complete* makes Bible reading easy by breaking down the entire Bible into 366 15-minute daily readings, arranged in chronological order.

Beautiful charts, maps, illustrations and diagrams make the biblical background vivid, timelines enable you to track your progress, and daily commentary helps you apply what you read to your life.

Why not get your church to read the Bible together in a year? Bulk discounts are available for churches!

Selwyn Hughes and Trevor J. Partridge
1,600-page hardback, 215x140mm
ISBN: 978-1-85345-433-2

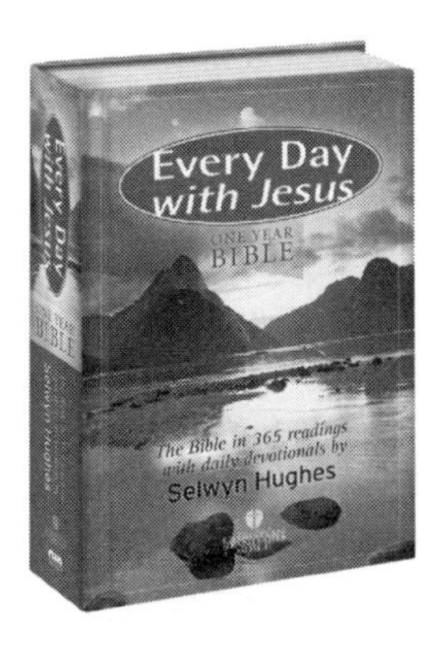


This deeply enriching way to read the Bible through in one year features 365 daily readings from both the Old and New Testaments, plus excerpts from the Psalms and Proverbs.

You will be highly motivated to keep on reading as each day's Scripture passages are made more relevant to you through devotional comments by Selwyn Hughes, a brief prayer and probing questions for meditation.

Why not get your church to read the whole Bible together with our Bible-in-a-Year Church Challenge?

Every Day with Jesus One Year Bible
1,594-page, hardback with ribbon marker, 140x215mm
ISBN: 978-1-85345-342-7

**This VOUCHER entitles you to obtain one copy of any 2011 issue of CWR's Bible-reading notes for 50% of the cover price.**

Redeemable at all participating Christian bookshops or direct from CWR, Waverley Abbey House, Waverley Lane, Farnham, Surrey GU9 8EP, Tel: 01252 784714.

Offer valid from 1 January – 31 December 2011. Valid in UK only.
**VOUCHER (GV1)**

50% off

---

**This VOUCHER entitles you to buy one copy of *Cover to Cover Pictorial Bible Atlas* (RRP: £11.99) for only £5.00.**

Redeemable at all participating Christian bookshops or direct from CWR, Waverley Abbey House, Waverley Lane, Farnham, Surrey GU9 8EP, Tel: 01252 784714.

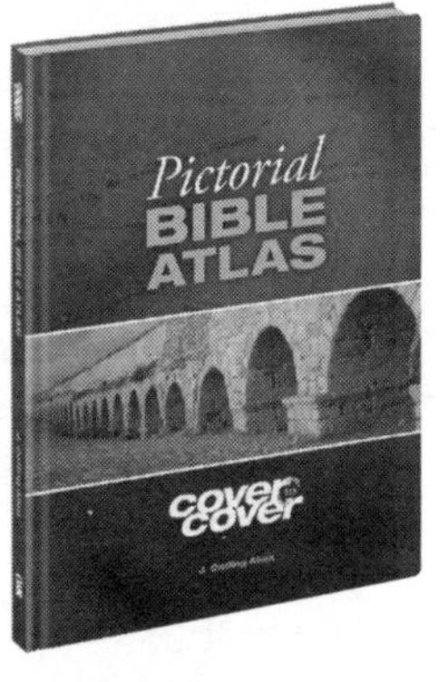


Offer valid from 1 January – 31 December 2011. Valid in UK only.
**VOUCHER (GV2)**

only £5

---

**This VOUCHER entitles you to buy one copy of *The Big Story* Bible-reading programme (RRP: £19.99) for only £14.99.**

Redeemable at all participating Christian bookshops or direct from CWR, Waverley Abbey House, Waverley Lane, Farnham, Surrey GU9 8EP, Tel: 01252 784714.

Offer valid from 1 January – 31 December 2011. Valid in UK only.
**VOUCHER (GV3)**

save £5

**Customer: Valid for redemption in UK only.**
**Only one voucher can be used against each item purchased.**

Retailer: Please return voucher to CWR, Waverley Abbey House, Waverley Lane, Farnham, Surrey GU9 8EP, by **31 January 2012** giving details of your shop and CWR account number. Your account will be credited less normal discount. Cash value: 0.0001p

**Customer: Valid for redemption in UK only.**
**Only one voucher can be used against each item purchased.**

Retailer: Please return voucher to CWR, Waverley Abbey House, Waverley Lane, Farnham, Surrey GU9 8EP, by **31 January 2012** giving details of your shop and CWR account number. Your account will be credited less normal discount. Cash value: 0.0001p

**Customer: Valid for redemption in UK only.**
**Only one voucher can be used against each item purchased.**

Retailer: Please return voucher to CWR, Waverley Abbey House, Waverley Lane, Farnham, Surrey GU9 8EP, by **31 January 2012** giving details of your shop and CWR account number. Your account will be credited less normal discount. Cash value: 0.0001p